A Second, a Hiccup

A Child's Book of Time

by
Hazel Hutchins

illustrated by
Kady MacDonald Denton

Scholastic Canada Ltd.

Toronto New York London Auckland Sydney
Mexico City New Delhi Hong Kong Buenos Aires

For the great-grandchildren of Peggy and Bill Sadler,
a delightful, ever-growing circle.
— H.H.

For Eila.
— K.M.D.

The illustrations for this book were created in watercolour and with pen and ink on Hotpress Arches paper. Gouache, charcoal and colour sticks were used to add different effects.

This book was typeset in 20 point Cheltenham.

Scholastic Canada Ltd.
604 King Street West, Toronto, Ontario M5V 1E1, Canada

Scholastic Inc.
557 Broadway, New York, NY 10012, USA

Scholastic Australia Pty Limited
PO Box 579, Gosford, NSW 2250, Australia

Scholastic New Zealand Limited
Private Bag 94407, Greenmount, Auckland, New Zealand

Scholastic Children's Books
Euston House, 24 Eversholt Street, London NW1 1DB, UK

Library and Archives Canada Cataloguing in Publication

Hutchins, H. J. (Hazel J.)
A second is a hiccup : a child's book of time / Hazel Hutchins, author ;
Kady MacDonald Denton, illustrator.

ISBN 978-0-439-94610-0

1. Children–Juvenile poetry. 2. Time–Juvenile poetry.
3. Children's poetry, Canadian (English). I. Denton, Kady
MacDonald II. Title.
PS8565.U826S44 2009   jC811'.54   C2009-901190-5

ISBN 10 0-439-94610-7

6 5 4 3 2 1   Printed in Singapore   09 10 11 12 13 14

A second

is a hiccup –

The time it takes
To kiss your mom

Or jump a rope

Or turn around.

A minute
is a longer time –

A happy, hoppy little song
Chorus, verses, not too long

Just enough to fill
A minute.

An hour
is a longer time –

If you build a sandy tower

Run right through a sprinkly shower
Climb a tree, and smell a flower
Pretend you have a secret power
That should nicely fill
An hour.

A day
is a much longer time –

Starting when the sun comes up
A day needs filling, like a cup
Hiccups, kisses, songs and showers
Lots of trees and lots of flowers

Breakfast, lunch and snack and dinner
Play some games and cheer the winner
Draw a picture, read a book
Tell a joke and learn to cook
Watch the sunshine fade away
Fall asleep, and that's a day!

A week

      is a much longer time –

Seven days make up a week
Sunday Monday Tuesday Wednesday
Thursday Friday and the end day
Saturday – a favourite one!
Some are quiet, some are fun.

Work days, home days, play days, school days

Seven wake-ups, seven sleeps

Close your eyes and do not peek
Still, you'd never
Ever ever
Stay asleep for one whole week.

A month

> is a much longer time –

A month is time for things to change
Seasons often rearrange

Winters melt and warm to springs
Caterpillars find their wings
And if you fall and scrape a shin
In a month there's brand new skin

Learn to tie your laces tight

Learn to float, relaxed and light

Learn to count clean up to ten
Learn to count back down again

Watch the moon grow round and fat
Then thin again, imagine that!
And all of it in one month flat.

A year
    is a much longer time –

A great big circle spinning round
Climb aboard, you're one year bound

You'll grow right out of your old shoes
And taller, too — now that's good news!

Sunshine, snow and rain and squall

Winter, Spring, Summer, Fall

Twigs on trees grow leaves and peaches

See how far a whole year reaches

Tiny babies learn to walk
Bigger babies learn to talk
Holidays of every kind
Linked together in a line

Now your birthday's almost here
And you are older
By a year!

A childhood

is a long, long time –

Hiccups, kisses, songs and showers
Running through whole fields of flowers
Laughing, learning, climbing, leaping
Building, dancing, reading, sleeping

Changes come and changes go
Round and round the years you'll grow
Till you're bigger, till you're bolder
Till you're ever so much older.

And through all the hours and days
As time unfolds in all its ways
You will be loved —

As surely as
A second
is a hiccup.